THE 12 MOST POWERFUL WAYS OF MAKING MONEY WITH UK PROPERTY

REGARDLESS OF YOUR BACKGROUND, EXPERIENCE, FINANCIAL SITUATION OR BUSINESS KNOWLEDGE

By Noel Cardona

THE 12 MOST POWERFUL WAYS OF MAKING MONEY WITH UK PROPERTY

*REGARDLESS OF
YOUR BACKGROUND,
EXPERIENCE,
FINANCIAL SITUATION OR
BUSINESS KNOWLEDGE*

By Noel Cardona

By Noel Cardona Copyright © 2022

First Printing: 2022

978-1-4583-5831-8

The 12 Moist Powerful Ways of Making Money With UK Property

Publisher: Property Cash flow
www.propertycashflow.co.uk

Disclaimer

The information in this book is for educational purposes only. The contents do not constitute financial advice in any way. You should seek Independent professional advice before making any investment. Investing in property can be a risky business just like any other investment. Historical growth in property prices does not mean necessarily that prices will increase in the future. Your property may be repossessed if you do not keep up payments on your mortgage.

To my little Isabella who, as of the writing of this book, is about to come into this world to make it a better place.

To all of you who are willing to do whatever it takes to reach your dreams through honesty, smart work and discipline.

PROPERTY INVESTMENT TACTICS IN THIS BOOK

INTRODUCTION

At a very high-level the property game is a very simple one: you get a property, either you buy it or control it, then you rent it as a single unit or parts of it, and then get a return. Hopefully, that return is a positive one once you take away all the expenses, such as the mortgage, bills, taxes, repairs, etc.

So, to begin with, that's your objective, **to create recurrent income and if possible, take more money out than you put in**.

Now, how do you do that? That's an entirely different story. There are different ways to achieve the same result as with any business.

There are many different strategies, many different ways in which you can go out there and get that profit, that cash flow, or those capital gains. In this book, I want to show you the main **12 different ways** which you can use to achieve such a goal.

Some strategies will require more knowledge but less cash, some others will require more time, you will find the ones that are more capital intensive, others will require less capital but more creativity.

It depends on the situation in which you find an asset that you want to acquire or control to get that positive cash flow or capital gain and this book is essentially a recipe, a tool, that you can use to get there.

Having said that, don't forget the most important part of the puzzle here, one you should never lose sight of YOU. It is you and your Quality of Thinking that ultimately make these property strategies work, not the economy, not the government, you. That is why to my students and investors I always say this: **You must grow the Property Investor First and Then Your Portfolio.**

You could grow an empire just to see it crumble if your level of thinking is not at all times higher than the needs of your assets. It would be like winning the lottery but losing all the money rapidly because you cannot administrate it properly.

Enjoy the book and if you want to reach me write to info@propertycashflow.co.uk. I will make sure you get a prompt response.

THE NOEL SCORE

In this book, I use The Noel Score which is the arrow symbols above for each strategy to give you, in a nutshell, how they score in complexity compared in general to all strategies in the book. It's a very useful way to know where you are and depending on your experience where you are more likely to succeed.

Let me explain what each item means:

Initial Capital: What initial capital you'd need to enter put this strategy to work before you get a profit compared to the others available.

Cash Flow: What level of cash flow compared to other strategies this model can bring. In the example above the strategy would have *Medium* cash flow compared to other models available.

Cap. Gains: The level of capital gains the strategy is likely to bring compared to others. In the example above you'd have no capital gains from that strategy.

C/XITY: Short for Complexity. It means how complex this strategy is to make a profit taking into account regulatory, building works, changes of use, etc.

Time: How much relative to other strategies this one is likely to take you as an investor until to get to profit as well as management.

Sales Mark: Short for Sales and Marketing. It's meant to show you how good you will need to be at sales and marketing to make the strategy work.

Exit: How easy is it to exit these types of investments?

You can have:

Arrows: Pretty much self-explanatory, High or Low, "Horizontal" for medium compared to other strategies.

You Are Here

On top of that, for each chapter, you will get a "property ladder location" for each tactic just to give you a feeling of the complexity like the one to the right. It can be the bottom, middle or top rung for easy, medium or high complexity.

WAY NO. 1:
RENT TO RENT (R2R)

INITIAL CASH CAP. C/XITY TIME SALES EXIT KNOW
CAPITAL FLOW GAINS MARK. HOW

Type: Middle Rung

Let's start right now with the first tactic…

The first way you can make money from UK property is called **Rent to Rent (a.k.a, R2R).**

You Are Here

This is a strategy where you don't own the property, you control it. This means you don't have to buy it and therefore it's not as capital intensive as other strategies, R2R and in layman's terms is this: you go to the owner of a property, explain what you want to do, secure the control of the

13

property and then rent it to several people on a room-by-room basis.

If you haven't heard about R2R and you are thinking, "Wait a minute, subletting in the UK is illegal!" I'd say… not really, if you have the consent of the landlord then it can be done. This strategy is used quite a lot and I am sure you have probably heard of "Guaranteed Rent" which is the use of it.

But before you gain control of that asset, you need to ensure the property is good enough to yield a positive return of at least £400 per month for you to make any money.

To do so, you need to find out how much you can charge per room according to the local market, then calculate approximate bills you will be paying (including rent to the landlord) and some 5% per month for repairs (this is a good management practice). If the numbers make sense, it's at least a green light to go ahead and contact the landlord.

Normally, in a R2R business model, you would pay all the bills because your tenants would be young professionals looking for an all-inclusive tenancy. People who are just starting in life, students for example.

Some gurus would say that you don't need any money for R2R but you do. You need to pay at least a month in advance in rent, at least a month of deposit and then you need to pay to adequate the property to ensure you can rent it out. In my experience for R2R, you need to have at least £5,000 to start with and be very clever in not spending too much money getting the place to look like a five-star hotel.

Finding Properties for R2R

To find properties suitable for R2R you have two options: one is you look for properties available for rent and call the landlord or the agency and discuss with them what you want to do, this way you need to expect that around 9 of 10 calls will become a rejection.

The second option is to use "sourcers" would you charge between £2K and £5K for connecting you with a landlord who is willing to work on this basis. The extra costs involved here will delay the time you start making a profit with this model but will save you time. Finding a good property is definitely one of the most important blocks of the process.

The Importance of your Due Diligence

Regardless of the strategy, you use to make money in property you need to know the rules of the game so you can set up each investment correctly.

In any business, you can choose to do things in the right way or become a cowboy. I certainly prefer the former. Let me explain what I mean with an example:

The screenshot below is from a sourcer and provides regular updates on properties available:

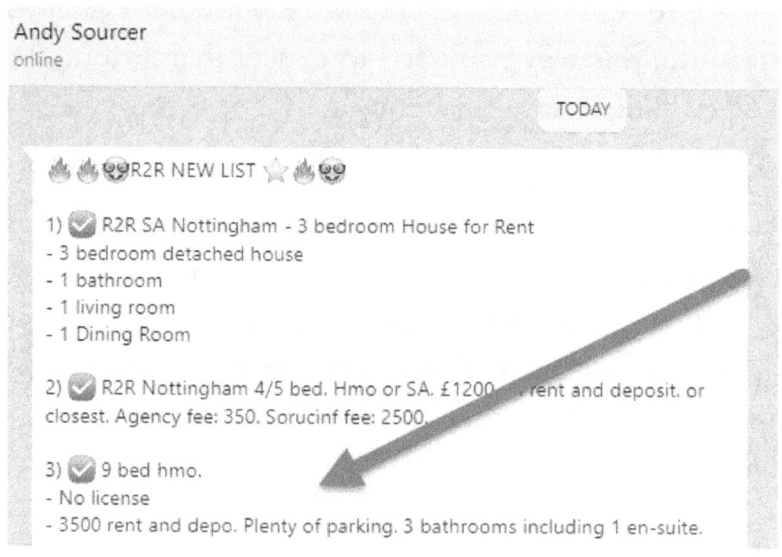

If you have a look at number 3 you will see that such 9 bed HMO (House of Multiple Occupancy, explained later on in the book) has no license and therefore you will need to know all the costs involved to get that license and apply for a change of use because a 6 people HMO is completely different, in terms of planning, than a 9 people HMO. Yet the majority of people buying that lead will just apply for a license and may get it but won't know they have created a "change of use" on planning grounds which will also require approval!

I've seen other people running these HMOs without licenses, which if the tenant is versed in the property world, can claim all the rent back from the agent (the one managing the property) by taking him or her to court.

The Mental Trap

Having said that, it is very important to pause and comment on the "5-start hotel" mental trap.

When somebody gets his or her first R2R, they more often than not miscalculate the amount of money they need to invest to get the place ready and they aim to take it to the level of "If I lived here, this is what I'd like the place to look like". That is not completely wrong because you need to present the room correctly, but you need to keep yourself in check to avoid going overboard with it and making your project fall into the red. You won't live there, so be careful how much you spend.

The Hidden Number

In any investment you do, there will always be the question of breaking even. That is, when will you get your initial investment back?

So, for example, if you put £10,000 into a R2R, to begin with, and get £500 net income per month, it will take 20 months (almost two years) to get your initial money back.

As you can see, your R2R could be giving you a good positive income each month and yet you would still be in the red (losing money).

That is why, as in any investment, you bootstrap as much as possible and do the best possible management of the property to avoid void periods which will just move your breakeven point further into the future.

A good rule to shoot for is a breakeven of 12 months, which means that in one year you have your initial money back in your pocket and are starting to enjoy the wonders of a positive return on investment along with cash flow.

Managing a Rent to Rent

Now, in terms of management, you're renting out rooms and therefore this is a management-intensive model, at least to begin with.

Once you get tenants which can stay for three months to one year, then you will have to take care of the repairs and other aspects of the business such as getting more R2R.

It is important, with this model, in particular, to keep the void periods (periods without one or more tenants) very low and that is done through a combination of good management, good tenants' recruitment and ensuring your "Client Service" is good for them to feel the property is worth their money.

R2R is not a single let where you just have to deal with one person, you are renting rooms separately, sometimes to single people, sometimes to couples. What this means is that basically, you will have more rotation of tenants, complaints about the behaviour of each other. Ultimately as I said more complexity but...

...that is the price you must pay for not owning the asset and just controlling it.

The "What if" fears

For the beginner, the worst fear R2R would create is the commitment of having to pay another rent apart from the one he or she is already paying. *"What if it doesn't work…? I'd be committed to a contract of 3+ years for a property? What if I can't pay it?*

Let me tell you a secret: the point at which you ask this question is the point where you either, start growing by going ahead or retrieve and become smaller looking for excuses and somebody to blame for your financial situation.

Only by facing your fears and taking action regardless, is when your Level of Thinking starts to increase and you get yourself out of the way.

The truth is that, if your R2R doesn't work (as it happened to many of the R2R during the 2020 pandemic) you just give the property back to the landlord or change your business model given you have direct contact with him or her. Just bear in mind you may be losing your deposit in that case.

Final Words on R2R

This book is not about going deep into each strategy but having a bird's eye view of the strategies available to you.

The R2R strategy is a model for those who have some savings they want to invest and can risk. For many is the first one that will make them property money.

This is a beginner's level entry model and what I've found during my time in property's that for people the two most difficult things to do in R2Rare,

First, to secure the property and,

Second, to manage their finances to be able to risk £5000 or £7000 and then make that investment work.

Behind the scenes, and always working against your own growth are your limiting beliefs and mindset trying to stop you from changing your current circumstances.

Wealth is not free and the main currency to pay for it is your personal growth.

WAY NO. 2: SERVICED ACCOMMODATION

INITIAL CAPITAL	CASH FLOW	CAP. GAINS	C/XITY	TIME	SALES MARK.	EXIT	KNOW HOW

Type: Middle Rung

The Second strategy is called **Serviced Accommodation** (SA).

SA has similarities with rent R2R but there is a big difference: SA requires a lot more management and time from your side than R2R unless you include a 10 to 15% in your numbers to get a management agent to do it for you.

You Are Here

In R2R, you would expect tenants to stay three to six months. In SA, you're expecting to see people stay from one night to maybe two weeks and therefore the rotation is higher, the check-in and check-out happen more often. It's effectively as if you were running a small hotel and as such, people will expect the service level, that is, the cleanliness and housekeeping to be professional. If you've ever rented an Airbnb, then you know what I am talking about.

CLIENT SERVICE

Nowadays, everything can be automated, but with SA there will always be questions from tenants which you may have not answered via your FAQs, so you (or somebody from your team) will need to be available to answer them.

An important aspect is how you manage the check-in and check-out processes. In this aspect, there are two different approaches: physical keys or electronic locks. The former could be normally managed by a key-box attached at the entrance of the property (disadvantage being that the code would be known unless you change it for each tenant which becomes a burden on its own) or you can use the service of local convenience stores who will charge a fee for key management where the guest will need to pick up and drop the keys). With electronic keys, you can supply a code and change it after each guest and this can be done from an app on your phone.

Also, you should work in tandem with your cleaners to inform you of any damages, even by using a checklist to ensure that your property is in pristine condition.

In SA it's important to take care of the details.

INITIAL CAPITAL

Assuming you are using property you control but don't own. You will require a month's rent and at least a month's deposit, so I would classify it as a mid-level in our Noel Score of making money with property.

If you are in London, you would be talking around £4K to £7K of capital to start.

A rule of thumb I use in the northwest of England is to calculate more or less how much you would have to invest to furnish an empty property is £1500 per room. This number includes kitchen and living room goods. For example, if you have a 4-room property you want to decorate from empty, then you would have to budget around £6000. Note that this number does not include painting only furnishings and white goods.

If you bought a property and want to turn it into a SA the numbers are heavily dependent on the size and location but once you've finished the refurb and costs above also apply.

CASHFLOW

Because of the short stay, you will be charging a lot more per night, depending on why the person is coming to visit and how the demand on the area is you could be talking from £150 to £300 a night in the peak days (known as "Event days") and between £50 to £80 in non-event days.

These numbers depend on the type of property, the location and the demand for it. The best way is for you to go to Airbnb input your postcode during weekdays and then during weekends. The latter tend to be event days however if your property is for example close to a stadium, a football match can make a weekday and very profitable event day where if the demand is a lot higher than the offer, you could be charging £500 to £1000 a night.

In SA the void periods tend to be on average two weeks per month so the numbers you calculate need to take that into account. When I do calculations on the profitability of a project, I use a 45% occupancy. If the numbers work at this rate, then you have a good safety margin.

In a way, SA is the "master of rental retail" as it can bring serious profits if you secure a property with a sought-after location and manage it with the Client in mind.

In an SA the biggest costs that will influence your profit are as follows:

a. Management fees: Up to 15% of your monthly income
b. Commission to marketing platforms (Such as Airbnb): Up to 15%.
c. Your Mortgage
d. Bills around 8%

See below for information, a screenshot for one of the properties I did my due diligence on:

Monthly cashflow (Serviced Accomodation)	
Average per room daily rental	£83
Occupancy	50%
Monthly income (A)	£3,750
Management Fee	£ (563)
OTAs commission	£ (563)
Electricity & Gas	£ (100)
Water	£ (30)
Broadband	£ (27)
Council tax	£ (140)
TV licence	£ (15)
Amenities and consumables	£ (45)
Other expenditure	-
Total Income	£2,268
Repairs allowance	£ (113)
Mortgage payment	£ (224)
Insurance	£ (30)
Net monthly income (B)	£1,901

CAPITAL GAINS

If you control the property but don't own it then you won't see any CGs. If you do own it, then you need to account for the fact that, as of the writing of this book, the valuation would be done as a brick and mortar and not as a commercial. However, lenders evolve day by day and having a good mortgage broker so you get up to date deals is a must in your journey to property success.

Needless to say, if you bought a property adding value then you will see CGs at the end of the process along with a good cash flow if you chose a good location.

COMPLEXITY

The complexity of SA comes from the fast-paced, multiplatform marketing and Client service you must put in. and that is after you've found a suitable property in a good location for the tourist type you are targeting.

Depending on where your property is located, you will need to take into account the regulations around the SA model. For example, up in the northwest, you don't need any licenses as they want to promote tourism, in London you can only use a property for SA for 90 days a year due to the lobbying of hotel chains that see heavy competition in SA properties.

As you will see later in more complex strategies, an important part of the property investor journey is to stay up to date with regulations (planning, building control, tax laws, etc) as they are evolving all the time. If you haven't done so, subscribe to my mailing list at www.propertycashflow.co.uk/subscribe so I can alert you through my emails and newsletters.

TIME

Compared to a R2R it will take more of your time, having said that, here is where you, as an entrepreneur of property must think automation, delegation, simplification. That is why I mentioned above the fees for a management agent who treats your property and clients in the best possible way and who does things according to current regulations as, the owner, is ultimately responsible for the safety of the occupants of the property.

Now, if you don't own the property, you will find that a 15% management commission will have a greater impact on your numbers and therefore you may have to choose to manage the asset yourself. If you are starting, that is not totally a bad idea so you understand exactly what needs to be done to have peace of mind that things are being done correctly.

SALES AND MARKETING

Whereas with R2R you could perfectly publish your rooms in one platform, with SA you need to do it multiplatform and have a way where you don't double book a property otherwise you will get bad reviews and that ultimately will hurt your business.

Before you publish your property on any of the platforms, make sure you get professional pictures taken as this is critical to enticing people to stay and pay you for the privilege.

EXIT

In my journey through Property, I've learnt to differentiate two types of exit: Plan A and Plan B. Plan A is what you buy or secure the property in mind: in this case using it as SA, if for some reason (a pandemic for example) that model stops working, then you will have your plan B, which could be single let or selling it/giving it back.

If you control the property and need to give it back to the agency or landlord before your contract ends, you will lose your deposit but you are not likely to have to pay let's say 2 years' worth of rent if that's what is left in your contract.

Until today, I don't know any agency or landlord you can be bothered to go to court to do that, they just get the deposit and rent the asset to someone else.

That was exactly what happened during the pandemic in 2020 as SA was one of the hardest hit and many entrepreneurs controlling many properties were forced to give them back. A friend of mind had to give back around 15 properties losing around £30,000 in combined deposits.

The bust was quickly followed by a boom in 2021 due to people having to stay in the UK for holidays due to the ban on international travel.

KNOW HOW

You could master SA within 6 months after you've gone through the process of getting your first one. From then on is rinse and repeat.

If you are just starting, start small, the SA model, even with a 2-bedroom property can give you a good return and provide you with the space to learn.

The most important for SA is to have: a good property in a good location, a good housekeeping team and good marketing to keep your void periods as low as possible.

Important not to forget about good client service to ensure your ratings are high.

WAY NO. 3: HOUSES OF MULTIPLE OCCUPATION (HMOS)

INITIAL CASH CAP. C/XITY TIME SALES EXIT KNOW
CAPITAL FLOW GAINS MARK. HOW

Type: Top Rung

The next way to make money from property is HMOs, which stands for House of Multiple Occupancy.

Like everything in business, there are different ways to arrive at the same place: you could run an HMO you own or you could you run it doing R2R.

In a way each R2R is an HMO because you have multiple people occupying a property, however when it gets complicated is when you intend to have more than 6 unrelated people in the same house (and this may change from council to council): on average, from 7 people upwards you will require more complex fire safety systems, planning and building control approval, this obviously will increase tremendously your refurbishing costs as well as increasing the complexity of managing the property as more people living together means more issues.

You could also buy a ready-made HMO of your own if you want to avoid all the hassle of creating one. There are specialised companies that put together these kinds of deals but…

…in this section, I'd like to talk about an HMO of your own that you create from a property that you buy. The reasons are explained below:

INITIAL CAPITAL

As we are talking here about creating an HMO from scratch, meaning buying a property, refurbishing it, getting it licensed, if necessary, getting it rented and managed, the capital requirements are high in the Noel Score.

Just to give you some numbers, at the time of writing this book, I bought a 5 bedroom property and turned it into an eight-room HMO. The purchase price was £115K, the upgrade costs were about £60K. So, as you can see, we are now a way off from the requirements of £7K to start a R2R.

CASH FLOW

One of the reasons HMO exist is because by renting a property by room, you get more cash flow than doing a single. You could say you would get between 10 to 20% more than a single let.

By the way when you hear the gurus on the internet telling you could get financially free with an HMO that give you £3000 a month be very sceptical and always ask whether that number is gross or net. If I assume is net, then the property would need to have a gross of £7,500 (£3K/0.4 with 0.4 being the net yield). That would mean you would have to have if you are charging £500 per room, a property with 15 people.

Having said that, before you decide between an HMO and a single let, do the numbers. The reason I say that is because, with a single let, the tenant pays the bills, with an HMO you as the landlord, do it. As it depends on each project, the management and effort required to have an

HMO may not be worth it when you can achieve similar results from a single let of a smaller property.

A way you can increase the rent you charge for each room is to create ensuites (rooms with bathrooms). By doing so you could charge between £50 to £80 more than average. The downside of doing so is that each bathroom will cost you around £2000 to £3000 to install. The upside apart from the increased rent is that by creating ensuites you can target a better tenant profile that will tend to give you fewer issues (professionals and students with higher income levels).

If your numbers can support a management agent then go for it but as I said before, do learn what requires to run an HMO legally so you audit the agent and make sure things are done property (Fire alarm testing, documents upon renting, gas and electrical checks, etc).

CAPITAL GAINS

Investing using this method can lead to high capital gains as the valuation is done on a commercial basis as a multiple of the annual income using a factor anywhere from 6.5 to 10. For example, the 8 rooms HMO discussed above, has a £2600 monthly income which is

£31,200/year. It was valued using a factor of 6.5 for £202,000. As it was bought for £115K it means the valuation was increased 75%.

The factor is decided by the valuer and using as reference HMOs sold recently nearby. If you get a factor of 10 you could easily have a deal where there is no money left in, in other words, you can recycle all your cash.

The massive increase in value comes from altering the layout so more rooms are added and proving to the lenders you are getting the type of cash flow we are talking about here.

This is one of my favourite strategies to create what I call Money Speed because you are creating value you can extract and then invest in the next asset.

COMPLEXITY

For an HMO, complexity comes with the territory and I say this because, before you plan to get into one, you must know whether the local council requires planning for it or even if they are allowed in that area. There is a piece of legislation called "Article 4" that gives each council discretionary powers to decide in which area they want to limit the number of HMOs. By using Article 4, they could decide that in just one part of a neighbourhood planning is required. That means you could have one street where on the right-hand side HMOs are allowed whereas on the left, they are not or require licensing. See the image below for an area of Liverpool which is where, as of the writing of this book I am investing the most, on the left of Walton Ln, there is no Article 4, but to the right there is.

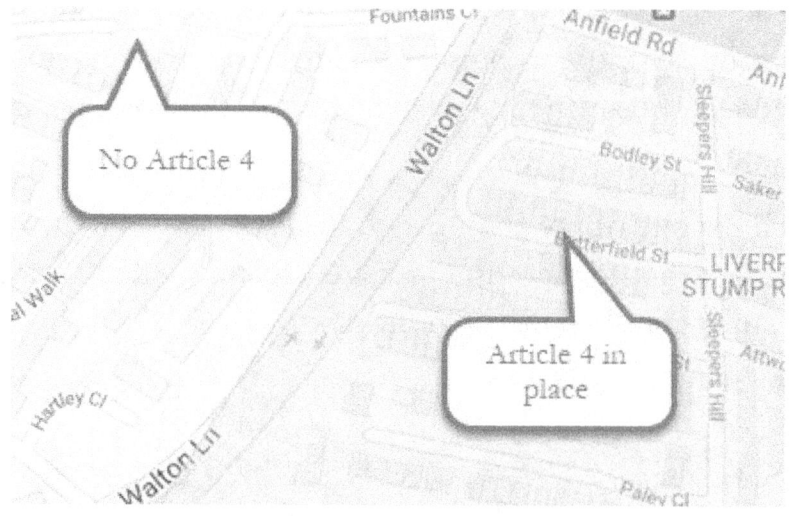

As I said before, complexity also comes from the requirements for fire safety. The more people you have living in a house the higher the risk of a fire starting the greater the risk to human life losses and the higher the likelihood of financial losses for you.

Councils work towards the quality of living and safety. This means that a good practice before you rent your HMO is to carry out a Fire Safety Risk Assessment. If the property you have been well designed or adapted to, you would have thought about fire doors, escape routes, emergency lighting and fire panel and testing, among others. Even though all that means less money in your pocket as a landlord and more management, also means you have peace of mind that your tenants are protected and you've done everything you can in case of an accident/fire.

TIME

If we talk about the management of an HMO, I'd say that once the property is all set up it would only need around 30 mins per week just to check that everything about the property is been done. Even if you have an agent, I'd advise you to check once in a while they are doing what they are supposed to and visit the property every 4 or 6 months to ensure your assets are taken care of. Nobody will care about your business as you do.

By visiting your properties once in a while (ensure access for inspections is authorised in the tenancy agreement), you check that, for example, the property is not turned into a crop house (cannabis factory).

A word or warning, when you are looking for an agent, it serves you well to have run an HMO yourself in the past, an HMO is an actual business and therefore it needs to be well administered. Take your time to recruit a good professional agent who follows all legislation: as the council personnel does not patrol the streets and rely on neighbour or tenants' complaints, it's all too easy to cut corners until you get caught up: Someone I know decided to run an HMO without a license after a year the tenants realised and took him to court winning more than £10,000 back from the rent.

What you could do if you have the cash but not the knowledge (and possibly not the time) to go through that initial setup you can contact me on info@propertycashflow.co.uk as I can get the whole process done for you.

The bigger the HMO, the more things are likely to break and more management is required. In that case, you can choose to do it yourself or pay a fee to an operator to run it for you (someone doing R2Rs) so you can get a guaranteed income. This means that your cash flow goes down but you get something more valuable back: time to go and build your next asset!

SALES AND MARKETING

Same as in R2R. I'd say the sweet spot for an HMO is 5 to 6 people (license is awarded on the number of people and not the number of rooms) so you don't get "problems of scale" with too many people living together which will be an objection from your prospective tenants.

Remember to decorate your property well and if possible, get the services of an interior designer as this is a critical step to make the property appealing and then take professional pictures staging the property in a manner that ensures you get tenants quickly.

By the way, also get good mattresses so your tenants have a good rest. They will be grateful for it. The marketing is done through the same platforms as R2R: Spareroom.com, Facebook Market Place, Facebook groups, roommatesuk.com, etc.

When marketing your rooms, you can either take a passive or active approach. What I mean by that is that you can just publish the rooms and wait to be contacted or use the platforms to contact people who 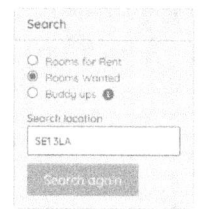 are looking for rooms in your area. In SpareRoom you can do this by using the "Rooms Wanted" feature.

EXIT

The bigger the HMO the more complex it could be to sell the property as some lenders might not have an appetite for them.

Having said that, if you have a licensed, well taken care of asset, yielding a good profit, you should not have any issues selling it as there is a healthy market for them.

If necessary, you could turn it into a Serviced Accommodation or Single Let model if for some reason you have to do so. As far as I know, you can run the property as an SA by still holding an HMO license (needs to be renewed every 5 years). Well-designed HMOs create very good candidates for SA.

KNOW HOW

This strategy has a lot of complexity to it. If you want to achieve the type of capital gains and cash flow that it can provide. If you have no experience, I'd advise you to get a mentor (I can help) or start small and very carefully so you don't end up making expensive mistakes.

The place to start is the council where the property is located or where you want to invest and then look, in the council page, the HMO requirements for that particular area. Each council has different requirements of facilities (Kent council requires tea point facilities whereas Liverpool doesn't), minimum living and common areas sizes, etc. Whereas all councils share common requirements you need to ensure you look at each of their requirement so you can get your asset licensed as required.

Something very valuable my experience has taught me about HMOs is that you would require three different levels of approval for an HMO: HMO License, planning approval and Building control. These are three different departments of the same council jet they don't seem to talk to each other. What this has created is a grey area where you can get an HMO license without having planning approval or building control. The problem is that you will get caught up when you are trying to get a mortgage for the HMO where responsible lenders will ask for such approvals and you won't be able to show them.

If you are caught in that situation, you will be forced to apply for retrospective approval which can easily set you back a year and cost you thousands of pounds if the building works have not been done up to standard.

If you want to start your property journey here, start with a very good mentor or start somewhere else.

WAY NO. 4:
DEAL PACKAGING

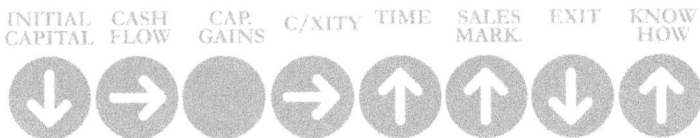

INITIAL CASH CAP. C/XITY TIME SALES EXIT KNOW
CAPITAL FLOW GAINS MARK. HOW

Type: Middle Rung

In the world of UK property, the strategy is sold as the one where everyone should start but I'd like to disagree and that is why I've set it a "middle rung" in my property ladder.

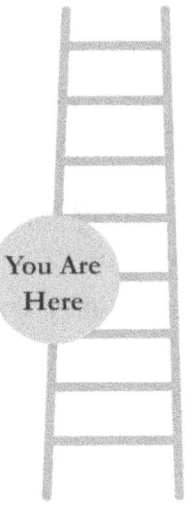

You Are Here

In basic terms, the way this works is by you specialising in a certain type of property asset or model and then finding business opportunities you can then pass onto other investors. You become a sort of a broker in this case.

I believe the key here is the word "specialise" because you normally have to know very well the market, the asset and the type of investor who wants that asset.

The last R2R I put into my portfolio is located near London Bridge, I paid him £2000 for the lead, and the property has been consistently producing £500 per month net and is about to break even. The fee can range depending on the property and normally is a fixed one between £2000 to £5000, sometimes more.

I recommend to my students they see this fee as the delay in months applied to their breakeven but is time that you save and therefore can use to find another property. Having said that, you can opt to become a good property finder and save yourself the fee.

Similarly, there are sourcers for all types of property deals. I, sometimes when I come across a deal and my hands are too full, pass them to investors and charge a commission.

INITIAL CAPITAL

You need almost no capital to start here apart from what you pay for phone and internet bills as you basically will be trading information and matching sellers to investors. The challenge is that, as you will see in the Knowledge section for this tactic, the trade-off and that you need to know the strategy and know what you are doing.

I'd say that if you have around £1000 in your pocket and good knowledge of a certain strategy then you can start here.

CASH FLOW

It will depend on how many deals you find, pack and sell, if you are good, you could be making anywhere from £3K onwards every time you close a sale. Like everything in business, it depends on you.

The cash flow will be created on the back of your hard work and you would need to take this tactic to a level where you have a team you can delegate the entire process of search and selling to be able to call this tactic one of passive income.

It is the lowest entry barrier tactic of all we are discussing in this book, but it requires the most ongoing effort on other fronts.

From my experience I've seen two types of sourcers, one is who negotiates properties regardless of location and then just send them to their investor list the other type is the one who gets properties and carries out some sort of due diligence ensuring the property does have a market, therefore, reducing the risk for the investor.

As an example of the first "no due diligence type", I got the other day this lead:

```
3) ✓ 3 Bed Mid Terrace House in
Bermondsey
 ! 2 Double 1 Single
 ! 1 bathroom is WC
 ! Front and back private gardens
 ! 2 driveways
 ! 5 min walking to Bermondsey Station
Rent: £2500
```

This is what you get and from here you need to determine whether the property will give you a profit. In the example above, having properties nearby (know the market rates) and without seeing the property I'd advise to make detailed due diligence to ensure if the asset would work for you: On top of the rent, you would be paying around £400 on top for bills, meaning that (£2500+£400+£500 profit)/4 rooms = £850 as average per room. Note that I am assuming there is a lounge you can convert into a room.

The second type goes beyond this and creates a due diligence sheet with a breakdown of major costs, set up mock tests to determine whether there is a market of the property, projected income and projected cashflow. At least they have put more thought into it and given you more information to the investor to evaluate risk.

It depends on you as a sourcers how far you want to go, my thinking is that if you do have a due diligence process before you try to pass any deals, you can then build a reputation for well-packaged properties and may be able to afford higher fees.

CAPITAL GAINS

As you are not selling property, there are no capital gains here.

Having said that, by working on these fronts, you will get to know the market very well and keep some of the deals for you, eventually getting CGs and cash flow.

COMPLEXITY

The complexity of this tactic comes from the business framework that needs to be in place to do it well at scale.

The systems required are the ones necessary to create a database of agents and landlords you can get your deals from and another one of investors who may be interested in those deals and then follow up potential prospects so you can close the deals. As of the writing of this book the market is very hot and active making it easy to package and sell deals. The more you can see all the numbers for the proposed strategy for the asset you found, the easier will be to sell. The reason I say that is this one:

There is lots of money to be invested in the market but the knowledge about a good property many times is not even with the closest to the asset, i.e., the landlords and the agents. If that wasn't the case there would not be properties in the market like the one below:

A two-storey mixed-use unit with a full first floor left to decay when it could easily be producing around £60K per year. If we were to assume that the landlord knows that, why has he not done anything about it? Probably because he is not thinking big enough or has no connections to get the money. In my experience, both are as likely.

Going back to your Deal Packaging Systems…

Within all the right framework in place, you will need to be available to answer enquiries as there are different levels of due diligence and some investors will ask lots of questions.

The other part of the complexity here is how you ensure investors won't bypass you and go straight to the landlord or seller. The normal answer here is that you get your investors to sign a confidentiality agreement as well as an agreement with the landlord to not deal directly with the investor before you get your fee paid and you should do that. However, there is nothing more powerful than the relationship you develop with those investors who will buy multiple leads from you as you know they are serious, understand and respect the work you do.

Having said that, don't just publish the full address of the property when attempting to sell the lead, otherwise dishonest investors will find a way to bypass you.

TIME

As you can see already, **time and knowledge** are the currencies you will have to pay by using this tactic. Not only that but also it requires discipline and consistency to be looking for deals all the time.

Being the UK a small island, it would be still very time consuming to be looking for properties you can package across the whole territory. That is why you need to choose an area of several cities or a big one which you can get to:

a. Develop a good relationship with agents
b. Get to know the best areas for properties
c. Get to know Council planning regulations in the area (article 4, conservation areas, selective license areas, etc)
d. Get to know the number of properties in the area
e. Get to know the best platforms for property marketing
f. Get to know the profile of the investor you will be selling to.

I could continue...

As in any business, as soon as you have the capital to delegate the processes you've created, do so, free your time and take your foot to the next rung up in the ladder. Don't be penny-wise, pound-foolish as the saying goes…

SALES & MARKETING

At least for me, the beauty of this tactic is that to make a living out of it and turn it into a tool that will add rocket fuel to your property toolbox, you need to become a true entrepreneur where the core of activities will be centred on Sales & Marketing.

I have seen it many times where, property beginners take the courses, go to meetings but fail because they are too afraid of the S&M activities. The normal response is to shy away and just keep dreaming about making it someday, about the financial freedom so many people talk about but few truly get…

To get an idea of how the S&M would need to work for you here, you just need to look at what agents do which is called "farming":

a. They specialise in a particular area (their farm)
b. They start marketing to landlords to get properties on their books

c. They are continuously, on the other hand, working to create a database of tenants who are likely to rent the property.

For deal sourcers, it's a little bit different based on:

- They are continuously working to create a database of investors who are likely to want the deals.
- When a good deal appears, then the pre-due diligence is done, the opportunity is packaged-up and then offered to their group of investors.
- There would be some terms and conditions describing the timings and conditions for the payment of the fee.
- If the investor gets the deal, then the deal sourcer gets the commission.

Even if you are just starting there is no excuse to start your marketing using social media, either organic or paid. But remember something critical: once you learn all the tools and paths you need to know to make the income you want, there will always be the battle of "consistent self-discipline" like Jim Rohn used to say, that is where commitment to creating the life you want shows.

EXIT

The exit for a Deal Sourcer would be more in terms of either stopping the sale of deals or selling the business that has been built around this tactic.

If you are a true entrepreneur and create the systems as you scale the business up, detaching yourself from it, then you could potentially sell it on and get a cash windfall you could use to invest in actual properties.

KNOW HOW

As I said at the beginning of this chapter, you can start with no money, but the more complex the type of deal packaging you are doing the more knowledge you will require.

If you are packaging R2Rs, then hopefully you know the details, can produce a financial forecast of the investment and test the demand so you can give all the facts to your investors and ensure the transaction is a win-win for all the parties.

If you are packaging an HMO, then you need to know whether the property requires licenses or even if in the area is allowed to have them operating. The final due

diligence is indeed the responsibility of the investor but…
if you spend most of your time packaging non-viable
investments, you will soon lose trust and no money will
come in.

If you are packaging a probate property, you need to know
about the process, if you are doing it with assets sold at
auction, you need to know the process… you get the idea.

WAY NO. 5: FLIPPING PROPERTIES

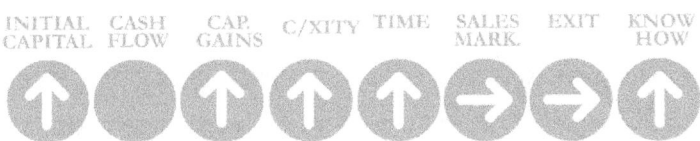

Type: Top Rung

Simply put, flipping a property is buying, upgrading and selling. Everything in between is details that you need to master and make this strategy work.

The ***buy low, choose the upgrade type and sell high,*** are the three unbreakable rules of the game. More about the upgrade type shortly.

I use "upgrade type" carefully because you could do "desk-based flips" that require no builders to be involved. These sorts of flips will be discussed later on. For this chapter, we can discuss the ones that do require changes in the property.

57

INITIAL CAPITAL

As of the writing of this book, the capital required will be at least 25% of the property's asking price plus what is required for funding the upgrade strategy.

Depending on where you are investing in the UK and the type of property, you would see that 25% translate into £25K or £250K or more.

In Liverpool, where I've been investing heavily in my own money, as of the writing of this book, I was finding good "flip candidates" properties for around £90K. Meaning, the 25% above would have to be £22.5K and then I'd have to get the rest via other means.

For a flip, a key part is to ensure that the type of financing you get (for your remaining 75%) allows you to sell the property quickly, or at least that it makes sense with the timelines you've set for each project. The reason I say this is because some high street lenders will place a "6-month period no sell" clause on the conditions of the mortgage seriously jeopardising what I call the **Property Cash Cycle,** in other words, how quickly you can get in and out.

That is why for flips, in particular, is important that you have a good knowledge of the type of lenders out there, some a faster than others, some have no-sell-clauses as above, some are more expensive than others, some won't like the type of tactic you are using, you name it. Given property investing is capital intensive, knowing who to go for quick financing is very important.

The following tip is very important and even more when you are in an area with a lot of competition. When you or your team goes to inspect a property, do it with pre-due diligence done and decide quickly if you will make an offer. At the time of writing, properties are flying off the shelves so to speak, and you need to make decisions quickly. Also, go prepared with a mortgage in principle from a lender and take proof of ID, certificate of incorporation (if buying through a company), proof of address, payslips and other proof of income. Look professional so your offer is accepted quickly and time is not wasted.

The Property Cash Cycle I mentioned above is very important, especially in flips and this is why:

Let's say you do a flip and get £25K net profit but it took you 18 months to do that the PCC is 1388 £. But another flip could have given you £10K in 3 months which is a PCC of 3,333 £/m. The latter project could allow you to make a lot more in 18 months than the former by recycling your money.

The PCC is important because when you start looking for properties you will have loads of options available to you and you will struggle to decide which to invest on. At that very moment you will need to use your investment criteria to make a decision:

Minimum ROI you would go for

PCC you would be happy with

Location (I calculate a Location Index of each property I see)

Cash left in the deal after refinance

…and any others you want to include. Don't buy using your emotions but a clear methodology that decreases the risk of you losing money.

"The second job of a property investor is to decrease the risk of losing money; the first one is to create cash flow."

CASH FLOW

Flips are not a tactic for cash flow, only capital gains. The reason is you have to get in and out as quickly as possible and therefore there is no time to get the property rented. For this reason, when doing your financial forecasts for your investment you need to include taxes into the equation as you could be paying around 20% in taxes from what you earned. Having a good accountant here is important because depending on the asset you want to buy (commercial, residential, land, etc) and the type of upgrade strategy you want to implement, your numbers will be completely different. For example, if you buy a mixed-use unit, the stamp duty you will pay will be much lower than that for a residential property, if you refurb a property instead of doing a new build, the VAT will be 5% and not 19%.

Remember that a successful investor is the one who can predict the numbers for the whole project the most precisely and for that he or she needs to know very well the process.

Your goal here is to create cash windfalls to fuel the creation of more cash flow generating assets which is what ultimately will give you your freedom.

CAPITAL GAINS

As I said at the beginning of the chapter this is a game about buying low, choosing the upgrade type and selling high.

If the upgrade type means refurbishing it where you would add rooms, extend, add bathrooms, etc means that you will need to ensure you reduce any markups from your builders and that the budget you set is followed closely not overspending.

A good tool for this is to join the Landlords National Purchasing Group (https://www.lnpg.co.uk/). A private company where you can, for a fixed fee depending on the number of properties you have (for example, the fee would be £198+VAT/year if you have 1 to 3 properties), have access to wholesale prices for many of the items you will use in the property.

If you are working on a big project and can afford a Quantity Surveyor, he or she will help you control costs, if not, you will have to do it yourself.

When it comes to flips, is never more important to do preplanning so you don't waste time or materials (hence money) in the process. Such preplanning can include:

a. Ensure you validate your numbers and use an accountant to take into account any taxes you will need to pay because of this investment and how you can minimise them by categorising correctly all the expenses in the upgrade.

b. Accessing the property before completion if possible so you check that the utilities are working. One of my properties didn't have gas installed and it took me almost two months to get it connected. Another one had the electricity disconnected due to what seemed a combination of issues and delayed the builders for a month before they could do anything that required work.

c. Ensure you have your architects and project manager on board so they can help you plan the project.

d. Getting the drawings done quickly before completion so we can have an exact picture of what you want to achieve: the layout of the rooms, walls to be demolished, electrical and pipework drawings, etc.

e. Create your Schedule of works before completion and chose a building that can do it on the budget you need to meet.

f. If you need, use building control to ensure that your Building Reg notes are created and your inspector is hired.

g. If you need structural engineers in the process then ensure they've done the calculations required.

h. Ensure that a contract has been signed with the builders

i. Ensure a Gantt chart or works timelines are agreed so you can inspect and follow up the timings to finish the project on time.

j. Ensure you deal with any planning or licensing required for the use of the project.

The delays can come from multiple places, however, don't allow the main one to be your lack of planning and organisation.

Looking at the property from a 10,000 ft view, any refurbishment project should be treated as we have described, however, a flip is less forgiving because you won't have the cash flow of the property helping you cover any expenses after is finished and the taxes applied are higher.

COMPLEXITY

Most of the complexity for this target is at the front and the middle. In other words, how to buy either below market value or with potential and how to pick the most efficient upgrade strategy and make sure it's followed to plant.

Your property's sale price will be dictated by whatever the market will pay for the upgraded asset you will have created by the time you are finished with it.

To ensure the numbers work, you either need to have a very close group of builders who will do the job with a combination of good, yet not so expensive, materials so the refurb doesn't eat all the potential profits or as some do, do the work yourself save the labour costs and mark ups. However, the latter will only work for small changes and will take away your most valuable asset: your time, which I always recommend guarding as close as possible and using it on the most important strategies you need to focus on which I describe in my book **"10 Golden Rules of UK Property Investing"**.

If you chose to give the refurb to your builders, then I would advise you still follow the costs of the refurbishment very closely starting with the material purchases and get at least two quotes for each so you know you are getting competitive rates and no mark-up is being applied in any way to them. This may be ok for other projects but not flips. Use the prices of the LNPG I discussed above to have a benchmark of what you would pay for example for a new boiler, kitchen, window, etc.

TIME

Time needs to always be recognised as more expensive than money.

Flips, as I've said will take more of your time and the project timeline needs to be compressed as much as possible so you get a good return (which is always a function of time).

If we talk about a flip that will take five to six months to complete, we would be talking, in normal conditions that:

a. You would be spending about 2 – 3 weeks finding a good property if you have already chosen your High Growth Area, or HIGA as I refer to it.
b. At least a month to complete the purchase (Auctions are 28 days). You are lucky if you complete a purchase in 28 days if getting it on the open market.

c. 4 to 8 weeks doing the refurbishment. It always depends on how complex you want to make it: the more you can add value the more profit you could potentially do. Bigger projects can take 12 months and even more if your strategy requires planning approval.

d. 1 to 2 months to find a buyer and complete on the property.

If it's a simple project, most of your time will be taken on the refurbishment stage. Do your best to keep costs down if you are doing the project management yourself and ensure the works are efficient and quick.

SALES & MARKETING

On my Noel Score, we set it to "medium". Selling and buying properties converted via flip is relatively easy if you have a good property, with a good location and in a hot market and a good agent. As of the writing of this book, properties are sold in less than two weeks some even the same day they come to the market and with multiple offers paying above the asking price. This undoubtedly is good for the flip strategy.

Normal channels can be used to make the sale such as Rightmove, local agents, Zoopla even Gumtree.

EXIT

If you've done your due diligence correctly as to location and rental demand, the works have been done to the right standards so you can provide the right certificates (planning permission and building control approval, fire systems for example, gas safe, Electrical testing, EPC rating, then exiting the flip shouldn't be that complicated.

Always remember, that unless you have a buyer who doesn't know much about a property with poor advisors, you are selling an asset that needs to pass investors due diligence: we all look to buy assets and not liabilities.

For example, at the time of writing this book, a new regulation came out where all properties need to have a fire risk assessment. What you get out of one of those assessments is a list of improvements that need to be done. If you upgrade the property and don't consider this subject (among others) then you will have created a problem by the time you attempt to sell.

KNOW HOW

This one is what would classify as an advanced strategy, where you need to know all the processes including refurb costs as well as how to work along with your builders to manage closely the project. Keeping costs down while creating a good sellable asset that complies with current regulations is the goal to achieve here.

As usual, you can do flips with small or big properties depending on your budget and confidence levels. The bigger you go the better you need to be at project management (even if you already have a project manager for the works) and the more you will need a team around you who can help you.

If you are just starting and want to get into flips then keep it small, ensure you work on projects that don't need planning permission and that can be easily managed. Then, on the next project, go for something bigger and stretch yourself.

WAY NO. 6:
TITLE SPLITTING

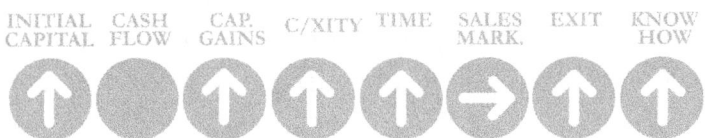

INITIAL   CASH   CAP.   C/XITY   TIME   SALES   EXIT   KNOW
CAPITAL   FLOW   GAINS   MARK.   HOW

Type: Top Rung

Imagine this: you buy a building with 12 big rooms. From those 12 rooms, you create the same number of self-contained studios and now you want to sell each individually. To do so, you need to legally be able to sell each flat separately and to do that you need to move from a freehold tenure of your property (assuming that's where you started) and the move of multiple leasehold titles, one for each flat.

You Are Here

What you then need to do is to "split the title" of the building into 12 leasehold units each belonging to a studio.

That's what is known as Title Splitting.

71

INITIAL CAPITAL

As you can imagine, is difficult to split the title of a 3-bedroom house, unless it has two stories and you can convert the ground floor into a shop or 1 studio flat and that you get planning permission to do so. So, title splitting requires high capital availability if you need to carry out building works to comply with the rules of this method.

Another potential way is that you find a property that physically has already been changed but the owner has not done the title splitting. These are rarer in the market but now that you know this strategy, then you can stay alert and potentially create one of the "desk-based flips" we discussed above, where you would buy the property, do the paperwork for the title splitting and then sell them individually generating a profit.

CASH FLOW

If we just analyse this model from a point of view where you bought the property do the upgrades and the title splitting and sell, then is a tactic with no cash flow.

CAPITAL GAINS

Title splitting is all about capital gains because normally by doing so, you would increase the value of each unit in comparison to just selling the whole building.

One way to determine whether a property could be viable to apply this strategy is to:

a. Find out the price of what each self-contained unit could be sold for and add them up.

b. If the ratio purchase to sell price is equal to or less than 75%, then you may have a good deal in your hands. The reason is that you will have some space to cover the costs of the process to use this strategy.

For example, a close friend of mine recently bought a property with 12 big rooms which he will convert into studios. This property is located on Everton Road in Liverpool. The market price he paid for it was £355K.

With studios currently selling for £50K in that area, then the calculation we discussed above would be:

$$\text{Selling Price for 12 studios} = 12 * £50K = £600K$$

$$\text{Ratio building price/Units sold} * 100 =$$
$$£355K / £600K * 100 = 59\%$$

This ratio means he has space to cover the costs of the title splitting and refurbishment work.

COMPLEXITY

This tactic can be as complex as the project above or as easy as a paper exercise as the example I gave before.

If you choose the above "desk-based flip", it will cost you roughly £1,000 to prepare a basic lease and then £250 to tweak it to fit each unit which being in the same building would be very similar.

If you go for more complex projects like the 12 units explained above, you will have to use your Trusted Team of builders, architects, planning advisors and lenders to make it work.

Also bear in mind that if you keep the leasehold units for yourself you will need to set up a separate company on which you own the freehold as the same entity can't be the owner of both.

As the freeholder, you will need to ensure the common areas are maintained which means you'll need to get your maintenance team to do this and create a different company you can provide the service from or hire a management agent.

Alternatively, you can also choose to sell the freehold.

TIME

Everything is a trade-off. If you want to focus on paper exercises then you will need to spend more time finding properties that are "leasehold ready". This would be the quickest way.

If you want to find a suitable property that needs conversion, it will be easier to find but would spend more time and effort on doing everything that is needed to get the project to work.

Of course, you can build a good network that could alert you of any potential property that fits your requirements so that it becomes more manageable to find.

SALES & MARKETING

The same toolbox to buy property you'd use for the other strategies applies here.

Market to owners of properties that may not be for sale and place good offers for the properties you identify which are suitable for the leasehold immediate creation or have such good potential they can give you a return of at least 25%.

EXIT

The exit on this strategy could be either selling each flat immediately and getting the capital gain, or you can get some of the money out by doing a re-mortgage once your project is finished, keeping the property and renting each unit.

If my friend wanted to do the latter with the property at Everton Road, he'd get around £7K per month of income and maybe around £250K from the re-mortgage which is a good sum he can reinvest on his next project.

KNOW HOW

Among many things you need to know how the Title Splitting process works. For example, you must remember that each self-contained unit must follow the minimum space requirements set out in the "Nationally Described Space Standard "which for example, for a 1-bedroom studio or flat needs to be at least 39 m² and not share any utilities with any of the other ones, otherwise they won't be mortgageable.

As part of your due diligence, you should ask these kinds of questions before you commit to buying, but if you find the right one you could have a pretty great deal on your hands.

If you want to start simple, you could find a home that already has been converted to two flats with only a communal hallway and then do the paper exercise, which will give you enough confidence to go ahead and do the bigger ones.

A very important part of the process is to get an expert to draft the leaseholds in such a way that you get additional income as the freeholder such as ground rents as well as very carefully specify what can or can't be done in the flats by the leaseholder.

WAY NO. 7:
BUYING AT AUCTIONS

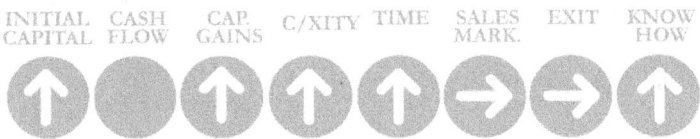

Type: Top Rung

Before I start, I am assuming here you are buying at auction, doing refurbing and selling. However, you could just as easily keep the property and rent it out.

You Are Here

Auctions are one of my favourite tactics to use but in its own right, it will only work in combination with other tactics if you want to achieve high returns.

INITIAL CAPITAL

This tactic is one of the most capital-intensive available. The reason is you must have 100% of your capital readily available or pre-arrange auction finance which normally comes more expensive than a mortgage (for example 4% vs 12% interest). Here is where having a pre-established relationship and knowing lenders comes in handy. However, is also important for you to know that, if you can afford the payments for the auction finance then you don't have to have all the cash in your account.

To bid for an auction you need to:

a. Get registered with the auction house you've found the property you want to buy. That registration process includes a debit card where you need to have ready 10% of the purchase price.

b. Read carefully the legal pack which is a series of documents such as licenses, auction house contracts, landlord statements and information, etc, so you know what you are buying.

c. Have picked your investment strategy so you can calculate what the maximum price you will pay is.

d. If you get the asset then you must pay 10% immediately if you win at auction and then the completion must be done within 28 days when you pay the other 90%. If you don't complete you lose your 10%.

Now, for the professional investor that money could come from personal funds, a fellow investor partnering with you or even a specialist lender who can quickly have funds ready for you for this situation. I've used the latter quite a several times because I have a very good relationship with several lenders who by now, know me very well and can help me use this type of financing.

As you can see, this strategy is very quick due to the 28 days deadline which gets everyone aligned and working to complete. I wish lenders and lawyers had systems good enough to complete every time in a month. If you are one of them, there is money to be made by giving a faster service to investors!

CASHFLOW

As auctions can be a tactic on their own (you buy and immediately sell if the numbers make sense) or a "tool for the tactics" where you buy a property and create for example a House of Multiple Occupation for cashflow or simply refurb and do a flip.

CAPITAL GAINS

The general perception is that auctions are used to buy below market value and that's partly the main aim but you need to be very careful. As these properties sometimes may be very rundown and may require a lot of investment you may be buying at a loss, for example:

You could buy a property for £70K which requires a £40K investment or you could buy one for £100K that is ready to be rented and produce cash flow. Which make more sense? Well among other things it depends on the current valuation of the renovated property. If the market price is £100K, then buying through auction and doing the refurb will be most likely leave the property in negative equity. That's why before you buy any property, you need to make the numbers.

Also, as of the writing of this book, the market is so hot that properties at auction are selling not far away from what the open market would pay for them. The effect is happening due to a lack of properties produced by a frenzy of investors looking for somewhere to put their money to work.

Another danger is the psychological hype of an auction where the offered price can just go to ridiculously high levels due to either newbies trying to get their first property or experienced investors who have identified value that you may not have seen and are willing to pay more to get the property.

That is why you need to make up your mind as to what is the maximum bid price that makes sense to you and at which you will stop bidding.

To calculate that number, you must have already your exit strategy in mind. Remember, as I've said before, exit doesn't necessarily mean selling the asset but the final purpose of it which could be renting it. Only by having such a picture, can you determine if the numbers make sense bidding limit for each property.

For example, let's say there is a 4-bedroom property you can convert to an HMO and can bet £24K annual income from it. If we assume that you get a valuation factor of 7.5 times annual income your property would be valued at £180,000. That is a commercial mortgage.

For that HMO you inspected it, took measurements and calculated your numbers so you know your refurbishing costs for the whole process, including auction fees, process costs and refurb costs is £60K. Then the maximum price you would be willing to pay for that property is £180K-£60K = £120K.

On the other hand, another investor who is trying to buy a 4-bedroom property for his family and who has calculated the brick-and-mortar valuation to be £120K and for the refurbishment has come up with a budget of £50K. She would be willing to pay only up to £70K.

Who do you think will win the action for that property?

The reason this book is so important is that to succeed as an investor you need to have this toolbox in your head and know what you are doing.

COMPLEXITY

Auctions are an advanced strategy, especially because of identifying the costs associated with upgrading the property to a level that can be sold or rented.

I know of an investor who bought a property at auction and who after removing a lot of vegetation from the backyard, he found it had a serious problem due to blocked drains that were making the property sink. This cost him a lot of money he hadn't budgeted for, but thanks to creative builders he managed to save the project.

Once you have visited and inspected several candidates' properties, then you need to have at least one or two as backups because is likely you won't win at first.

Once you win, then you need to work with your lawyer to ensure the completion is done within 28 days. Lawyers are used to this so this is normally not a problem.

Then the refurb stage starts for which you need your team of builders. Properties that tend to go to auction normally require quite a lot of work although this is not the case every time.

One of the main points of complexity is that of reading and understanding the legal pack, trying to find what is potentially wrong with it. If you go to any auction house where the lots as they call the

Document
CONTRACT-20 Bingley Road.docx
Official Copy - Register.pdf
Fittings and Contents Form.pdf
Official Copy - Title Plan.pdf
Common Auction Conditions 4th Edition (Sept 21).pdf
Notice to Prospective Buyers.pdf
Online Auction Buyers Guide.pdf
20 Bingley - EPC.pdf
Property Information - 20 Bingley Road.pdf
COMMON AUCTION CONDITIONS (Third Edition).pdf
HMO Licence.pdf

properties are advertised before the auction then, you will find that a legal pack looks like something like the picture above with a different document to download. It's very important that you as an investor:

a. Understand the fees involved to buy from the auction house
b. Understand any defects that the property can have
c. Visit and inspect the property trying to look for a reason for NO to buy.
d. Talk to a lawyer if necessary to help you review the legal pack
e. Anything else you can do to find, again, a reason NOT to buy.

TIME

As you can see getting this strategy to work requires a lot of time. Especially because you the work mentioned with the Legal Pack. For example, at the time of writing this book, I've been waiting for around a month and a half for a property which upon inspection I discovered was a "Crop House" where the tenants or owners were growing cannabis. This is a good property but it's taking a long time to be ready to be sold. Once I get the legal pack, I will need to do my due diligence to ensure there is nothing that will affect my decision but hopefully, it gives enough time before the auction to do the due diligence and remember, the legal pack can sometimes change so you need to keep an eye on it.

Having said that, the extra time you use in due diligence is buffered by the 28 days completion period.

SALES AND MARKETING

To buy properties in the auction you don't need to have great M&S skills (Compared to the strategies where you want to control an asset without buying it) apart from having your due diligence done and having the psychology in place to respect your bidding limit.

Many auction houses specialise in advertising and selling properties via auction. There is one in particular that put together all auctions in the country: www.eigpropertyauctions.co.uk. So that would be a good start for you to explore.

The property can then be sold at any time once is yours via the normal channels such as landlord contacts and the open market.

EXIT

As we said before, by the time you buy, you must have your exit strategy in mind otherwise you can end up with an asset with negative equity and even though the property may correct this issue with price increases over time, is not a good position to be in.

KNOW HOW

This is an advanced strategy where you will need the support of your Trusted Team especially your lenders, lawyers and builders.

To use it, I'd recommend you try some of the ones "bottom-rung" type first so you know that your exit strategy is possible.

WAY NO. 8:
FRACTIONAL OWNERSHIP

INITIAL CAPITAL	CASH FLOW	CAP. GAINS	C/XITY	TIME	SALES MARK.	EXIT	KNOW HOW

Type: Bottom Rung

Compared to some of the strategies around, this one is relatively new. In very simple terms, it's similar to owning shares in a piece of property and it has been made possible thanks to financial start-ups using technology to sort of create a property stock market where it's easy to get in.

You Are Here

INITIAL CAPITAL

You can start with as little as £100 to get a fraction, a share if you wish, of the property.

One of the companies that do this is propertypartnet.co (I have nothing to do with that business by the way) and I just show it as an example for you to know what is possible.

The whole idea for this model is to pool small investors together so finance can be raised for new properties or to create a new form of exit for these investors after they bought one. It has some similarities to crowd funding but is not entirely the same.

Before you get into this tactic, I'd say you look very well at the entry fees they will charge you as that will affect your investment forecast. The best way of doing this is to read through their documentation, talk to an advisor and only start very small so you understand how easy is to get out.

Having a look at the full cycle of the investment before you commit a considerable amount is a good idea here.

I put £200 in one property so I could learn their business model but the property since has decreased in value and I've made a £60 loss. That is the importance of starting low.

Do serious due diligence before you commit substantial amounts of money to this strategy.

CASHFLOW

One of the biggest differences with crowdfunding is that this type of strategy will allow you to get some monthly cash flow as you effectively have some equity in the property. The problem is that as you only own one part of it, you only get a small part after fees.

For my amazing investment of £200, this month I got:

Monthly income

£0.34

Dividends received

I may not be able to retire on that!

CAPITAL GAINS

As this system is effectively a stock market for property ownership your capital gains will come from an increase in the share price of the property.

Given that this system allows you to get in and out relatively quickly, it can make the share price fluctuate more than if you were buying an actual property.

That is why you need to be careful and "play" with the system until you feel comfortable with it.

A graph of my £200, shows that seemingly due to Covid there was a decrease in the property price:

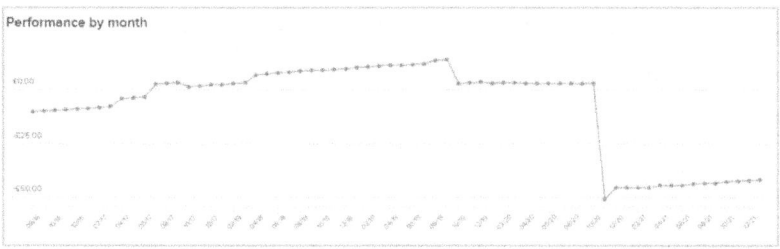

Something I've noticed with this strategy is that this system seems to react a lot faster to changes in the market as opposed to actual property.

COMPLEXITY

More than anything the complexity here comes from understanding the dynamics of a "Fractional ownership property stock market" which is essentially what I've been describing here.

Getting to understand how much is going to cost you to get in and how much is going to cost you to get out is very important and also, doing quite a lot of due diligence to invest in high growth areas, which by the way, if you get my daily emails, market updates will be regularly sent. (Send me a note to info@propertycashflow.co.uk so I can add you to my inner circle list).

TIME

You will need some good time invested to understand the platform and then to choose the areas which are growing the fastest. From then on, you will need to monitor your investments regularly.

When you are dealing with stocks of any kind, please bear in mind that if you start worrying about the daily ups and downs of prices, then you may have a hard time holding such investments, I'd say focus on the dividends coming in and don't check the stock price too often.

SALES AND MARKETING

Using this tactic, you don't have to talk to anybody so the S&M skills you need here are very basic. You'd need more to develop your analytical ones. That is why I say this is a "Bottom Rung" strategy in my UK's property ladder along with the fact that you don't need much capital to get it.

EXIT

You can exit this kind of investment by selling your shares or by something called the "Five Year Exit Mechanic" in which the property is valued and the price of the shares updated as per a new market valuation.

That is why I say the exit from this tactic is of mid-complexity: you could sell your shares or wait for longer until the five years mechanic. Exit strategies will change for each platform so start your due diligence from scratch for every new one.

KNOW-HOW

Having the patience to find out High Growth Areas and ensure you understand each platform is very critical.

Here you don't need to deal with lawyers, tenants check-ins or check-outs, builders or lenders but you need cash and the chances of getting a loan (unless unsecured) to invest using this tactic are very slim.

WAY NO. 9: CROWDFUNDING (As Client)

Type: Bottom Rung

I'd say that if you want to start in property but have very little funds, not much time and not much experience, looking for a good property based crowdfunding platform is a great place to start.

Crowdfunding is companies authorised and regulated by the FCA to take the money of many small investors and invest it to get a return. Nowadays there is a crowdfunding company (CC) in almost every industry and property is not an exception. It's been one of those breakthroughs created thanks to the powers of the web.

Like in the Fractional Ownership tactic explained in this book, crowdfunding has been a core strategy to get investors and then add some additional complex layers to make money.

INITIAL CAPITAL

You can start with very as little as £500 depending on the platform; you could invest in multiple projects in different areas.

Remember that what you are doing, in general in crowdfunding, is lending money to builders and other property investors, with the crowdfunding company as the intermediary, and getting interest on the loan, you are not getting equity (which is the difference with fractional ownership or actually investing in property).

CASH FLOW

Because you are lending money to other investors, the interest rate (which determines your cash flow) competes with the rates many other lenders are offering, so if the crowdfund gets to work on high-interest loans (such as bridge loans) then they can produce a good return on your money. Obviously, take into account that the CC will take part of that interest so if they charge let's say 10% to the borrowers you may just get 6%.

The way most crowdfunds make their money is by the fees they charge the borrowers which can be paid upfront by them or added to the loan. Although normally the individual lenders funding each project don't get charged any fees, this may change from platform to platform.

You would normally have to lend your money for a fixed term (at least 6 months or a year) and then get a monthly payment based on the interests agreed. You get your capital back at the end of it.

One CC I've used in the past is called lendinvest.co.uk. (I have no financial interests in this business). This fund requires at least a £5000 investment and would provide between 6 to 8% annual ROI on your capital.

It is important to understand that even bottom-rung tactics like these are capital at risk. If for example, the lendee doesn't pay interest or capital, you may not get your capital back for a while until the property is repossessed via the first charge that will be put against the security. In other words, for the lendee to get the money, a loan is recorded against the property and the lender can claim ownership if the money is not paid back.

Also, crowdfunding is a business and if it goes bankrupt then your money can also be lost.

CAPITAL GAINS

You are not getting equity so there are no capital gains in this tactic.

COMPLEXITY

The complexity in this tactic as a client is low because the crowdfund takes over all the due diligence using their trusted team to effectively ensure the lendee return the money plus interest.

Your job as an investor is to ensure that you pick a solid business with a good reputation, especially because if you are using this tactic, you may not have high-risk tolerance as the Renegade Investors (as I call the ones in my inner circle) who are using top the ladder tactics.

Remember that the crowdfund must be authorised by the Financial Conduct Authority.

Always start with a small amount to understand more the business you are getting into, do your due diligence, find out how much they've lent and find some good reviews if possible. Talk over the phone, if possible, to somebody who has invested there.

TIME

In my experience this tactic requires even less time than the fractional ownership one as I said, by choosing a crowdfund with a good track record then you would be able to have more trust in each project they propose for funding.

SALES AND MARKETING

You don't need any of those skills here which makes it easy to start with this tactic.

EXIT

When you choose a project to fund (from different ones always available) you will be informed about the term of the loan and that is the time that your capital will be tied up. You won't be able to exit your investment until that deadline.

Having said that, if the lendee decides to extend the term of the loan you will have to wait for longer or if the loan is paid earlier then you may get it sooner.

The reason for the above is that crowdfunding works quite a lot with bridging loans which are short term (6 to 12 months loans) with high interests, i.e., 12% p.a. in comparison to 3% of a bank as of the writing of this book. If, for example, the builder has planned to finish a development in 12 months and delays in any of the parts of the process happen (not uncommon), then the bridge loan will have to be extended and therefore your money may be tied up for longer but getting a similar monthly return.

KNOW-HOW

For each project you want to fund, you will get a report with all the documentation necessary to understand the due diligence done on that project, is a good idea to study each and decide because, even though you place your trust in the crowdfunding business, it's ultimately your responsibility.

Also, understand that the income you get through this tactic is not net tax and you will have to declare it via your tax returns to the HMRC.

WAY NO. 10:
CROWDFUNDING *(As an Owner)*

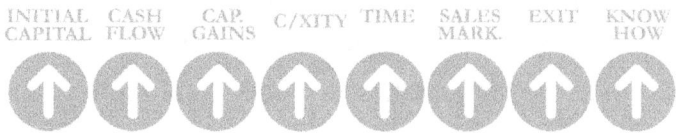

INITIAL CASH CAP. C/XITY TIME SALES EXIT KNOW
CAPITAL FLOW GAINS MARK. HOW

Type: Top Rung

When you have made your way through the Property Investment ladder and you have full command of the tactics, strategies, have a well-trusted team and have very good business skills, this is the strategy to follow: raising finance at a professional level and joining the investors who have mastered this tactic to enjoy "finance raising on demand".

You Are Here

This is an advanced strategy and will require everything you know in business to make it work.

INITIAL CAPITAL

We are talking about setting up a business here which will use all your knowledge and the one from your Trusted Team to make money in property by servicing builders, developers and individuals who are investing in physical properties. As such, you will need seed capital to set up the initial structure which allows you to break even as soon as possible and make it profitable.

Among those costs would be to get approval from the FCA (between £600 to £15K and could take around 12 months), marketing systems and creating the actual crowdfunding platform (website) where you can gather your investors and present the different projects.

If you've done well in property, you should have a good cash flow to support the growth of your crowdfunding platform until it gets profitable, which could easily take 3 years.

CASH FLOW

As with any business, it depends on how big you wanted to get and therefore how much cash flow you want to generate. Again, we are talking about a business that is benefiting from a deep knowledge of the property market, together with the leverage of good marketing systems and a well-established Trusted Team.

As this business would be making its money from the fees charged to borrowers, for example, as of the writing of this book a bridge loan of £350K, would be charged 0.75% monthly with 2% arrangement fees (£7K). If you wanted to make a million pounds a year in gross revenue from this tactic then you'd need to be getting circa 140 borrowers.

Crowdfunding is a great way to turn information and good marketing to profit which could be re-invested into more property.

COMPLEXITY

Very high complexity as we are talking about a business where you will require all the common operating blocks such as marketing, legal, property experts and finance. Not something you want to do alone.

Having said that, you can look at outsourcing as much as you can until there is enough cash to bring it in house.

By now, there are lots of crowdfunds for which you will have to compete in service and rates, so it doesn't get any easier I am afraid.

The question you may ask is, why on earth if the Property business is meant to produce passive income and get the investor free time, would somebody get into one of these?

Well, my experience is that the property investors that make it to this level are true entrepreneurs who are aiming to achieve new heights all the time, for some is not about the money anymore but about creating a legacy or helping others who want to have big portfolios. Crowdfunding is a good way to turbocharge that journey.

True entrepreneurs enjoy the challenge and taking a property to this level may be something they are naturally attracted to.

TIME

As a property investor and business owner, you should look at creating a business joint venture here so the weight of this strategy doesn't fall on your shoulders. Ideally, you should team up with somebody who has experience in the lending, property and marketing areas.

Setting up a business is never easy and you need to ensure you allocate the necessary time to get this done.

A potential strategy to save you time is to use a "White Label" crowdfunding platform. What this is, is a ready-made platform that will help accelerate the process quite a lot for you if you don't want to start from scratch (which, really you shouldn't). This comes with a monthly cost of around £3K but some already come with an FCA approval for the platform. Find more info here: https://www.whitelabelcrowd.fund/. (Again, I have no financial interest in this platform).

SALES & MARKETING

A top rung type strategy like this normally requires very good S&M skills because you need to do the normal exercise of creating a pool of borrowers and another pool of investors (lenders) and both will need separate marketing campaigns.

Marketing is the heart of a business and needs a tremendous amount of work and especially a lot of cash and connections to make it work.

A great thing about this tactic is that once you prove trustful to an investor, then you would have repeat business and plenty of available funds to match to good property projects.

EXIT

The exit strategy here is, like in any business, either put in place a management team that requires no input from you or sell the business for multiple once it has enough proven revenue.

It all depends on where you come from on your property journey and how you want to diversify your investments.

Once you built an asset like this you will have a good source of finance which could benefit other projects you may be working on.

KNOW-HOW

To use this tactic, you need to have graduated from the property and business journey. Many crowdfunding businesses thrive in the "short-term high-interest loans" field as they can offer attractive rates to investors and facilitate the investment process for builders who need bridging financing.

If you have not tried the bottom or middle strategies (and even many top-rung types), please do so before you get into a tactic like this, as every bit of experience you gain will help you towards the due diligence that needs to be done to ensure developer and investors looking to get financing to have a solid model and are likely to pay the interest and capital back.

WAY NO. 11:
JOINT VENTURES

INITIAL CAPITAL	CASH FLOW	CAP. GAINS	C/XITY	TIME	SALES MARK.	EXIT	KNOW HOW
⬇	➡	➡	➡	⬆	⬆	➡	⬆

Type: Top Rung

Let's imagine you want to invest in property but don't have the money to do it. What do you do?

You Are Here

Well, if you know where to find properties, how to add value, how to comply with planning, building control, licencing, permitted development, etc., then you have what is required to do a joint venture, where you could put the intellectual capital and your time and then other investors will provide the cash.

Due to the knowledge that you require, I have classified this tactic as a top-rung type.

INITIAL CAPITAL

In JVs, there are two types of capital, one is cash and the other one is intellectual. You may ask the question why would on earth somebody share their hard-earned cash with somebody else by giving up equity in a project?

Well, that is a good question. As you go into Property you will notice the following pattern, there are more people with cash in the bank than people who know what to do with it. So, if you develop a reputation for creating good projects that comply with the necessary regulations and generate a return that can't be easily found in other fields, then you should be able to investors for JVs.

As per our arrow's indicator, we have set a low requirement as for your, the JV creator wouldn't have to provide much cash. Each JV is a particular agreement that could mean one investor provides all the cash or all parties provide different amounts with the one providing less adding intellectual capital to the mix.

Alternatively, you could be the investor who doesn't have a deep knowledge of property and find a person like me to help you advance on your next property project. If this is the case, remember this piece of advice, try to learn at least the basic pillars of each investment so you know your partner is doing everything as it's required per law and so you can assess critically that things are being done correctly. For example, if you are creating an 8 people HMO you must know that a planning application to get a Sui Generis approval as well as the fact that such a project requires a lot more complex design and building control approval than a simple buy to let.

CASH FLOW

A JV can be set up to create capital gains or cash flow, it varies. In the JV agreement, which I recommend is done in writing, the exit strategy should be set out explaining future the spilt of profits or cash flow. For example, if the JV is going to be for a flip, are the capital gains going to be split 50-50? If the JV is for an HMO, is the monthly cash flow going to be split 50-50? Who will do the management? Who will be the company director if the property is bought through a business?

CAPITAL GAINS

For the uninitiated, the capital gains for the person putting the intellectual capital would be infinite, and that is partly true but knowledge capital requires an equally important resource which is time. You see, each project has a lot of management and if you are the one doing the leg work then it means a tremendous amount of time will need to be invested.

COMPLEXITY

An unexpected piece of complexity and I'd say one of the most important ones, is the core value alignment among the investors in a project. Finding people who match your work style and beliefs is not easy. What I mean is that there are lots of cowboys out there, breaking all kinds of laws and not following any guidance, trying to make a quick profit without caring too much about the final client (Tenant).

I love it when I see responsible landlords, builders and investors who want to do things correctly and make an effort to create a better project each time. Why is that important? In my view, you want to build a portfolio that is strong from the ground up and allow you to sleep well at night.

What I mean by that is that for example, if you set up an illegal HMO, councils have 10 years to find out and correct the whole thing or shut it down. The same thing for a conversion of a building into flats.

Worse if that HMO has no fire safety measures and an accident happens, then you would be in a very bad position in court.

TIME

I mentioned before a JV is there because:

a. One investor has cash but no time or knowledge
b. The other one has time and knowledge but not cash.

This is very common in the UK and other parts of the world.

Savings are not the most valuable type of money and the knowledge-time mix is as valuable as those savings. Hence the importance of JV.

The investor providing the cash should only spend around 5% of the time invested in the project whereas the other investor will have to deal with milestones such as:

a. Finding a suitable property in an area where the target strategy is viable

b. Competing with other investors to get the property as there is tons of competition out there.
c. Setting up a business and a JV agreement
d. Find lawyers
e. Find financing
f. Find builders and project management, if he won't be doing it himself.
g. Find building control
h. Find planning approval
i. Find architects for drawings.
j. Ensure all works are done properly
k. Once the project is done, find refinance
l. Find new lawyers
m. Find an agent for management or sale
n. Ensure all certificates and approvals are in a file

You can see what I mean and how intellectual capital plus time is so important here.

SALES & MARKETING

If you have the time and knowledge but would be asking how you can find investors to start creating JVs, the answer lies here.

There are two ways in which you can do Sales & Marketing:

a. One to one
b. One to many

I am a big believer in leveraging through systems so your efforts can be multiplied. I am talking about the "One to many" type of marketing as it's very powerful. If you are truly serious about making Property a business for you, immerse yourself in the subject of Direct Marketing.

"One to one" marketing such as going to networking events is also useful but you can hardly automate that process. The "One too many" can be, with a good amount of effort, be systemised so you can have a constant stream of leads coming to you.

Of course, you can create JVs with relatives and friends, but depending on the size of the portfolio you want to create, you will soon run out of those investors and will have to get out to the world to find new ones and when you try to do that, you will find that the most valuable resource in business is Trust. The trust you will need to create between you and other people so they decide to invest with you or lend you the money.

EXIT

The exit should be established on the JV agreement. It could be a flip through a business which then can be shut down (remember to pay taxes on capital gains) or keeping such business open to invest in more properties and create a portfolio of flips and properties for cash flow.

As long as the investors are aligned, then things should work well.

KNOW-HOW

I'd say JVs are better posed for more complex projects. If you have the cash and want to do a simple buy to let to a single-family, you should try and do it yourself. But if you are going to get into Serviced Accommodation, HMOs, complex conversions, then find a JV who can prove he or she can deliver.

The game of property is beautiful because all projects have common stages and once you've worked through a complex enough one, you will be able to navigate the complexity of the UK's property market.

Don't underestimate the value of the Knowledge-Time mix as it's as valuable or even more than cash.

Also, don't underestimate the importance of asking questions if you are the one providing the money. The 5% of the time you invest should be used mostly for due diligence and making sure, based on facts, that the JV partner can deliver. If the project fails, then you will have a financial commitment and a personal financial guarantee that you would have had to give to your lenders in case you can't make the payments.

WAY NO. 12:
LEASE OPTIONS

INITIAL CASH   CAP.   C/XITY TIME SALES   EXIT   KNOW
CAPITAL FLOW   GAINS   MARK.   HOW

Type: Middle Rung

Lease options is a strategy that can be used to facilitate the purchase of a property for you by giving time to get the funds required or one that can be used to create a capital gain by locking the property and then finding a buyer as soon as you can.

You Are Here

INITIAL CAPITAL

With a Lease Option you could buy a property for £1 (as the lease would require some money being interchanged), such money transfer would be done on the signing of a Lease Agreement that I would advise you to get drafted by a lawyer.

The lease will have a deadline by which the option to buy will expire (it could be 3 to 4 years) and therefore by then, you need to either get the money or sell the lease to somebody else. In the meantime, you will have to pay rent to the landlord as you will be controlling the property.

If you decide to buy the property then the investment would work as normal depending on the type of asset you are buying. You may have an advantage though: if you managed to get a lease option on the property you may have had some room to negotiate the prices better than if you had bought it in the open market and therefore could be paying prices below market value (BMV).

Let's say, for example, you negotiate a property whose market value is £100K to be bought for £90K and the least is for 3 years where the market value could be £110K. Then you would be buying £20K BMV.

The disadvantage of this property is the speed of it because generally in 3 years you could buy several properties recycling the cash more efficiently.

If this is your first property and you want to lock the deal and allow you some time to get the cash then is not a bad one.

CASHFLOW

As I've said, the lease option may come with the commitment from you to pay rent, cover financial commitments or any other some sort of arrangement with the owner as he or she needs to get something in return for the asset.

Each Lease Option is different depending on the circumstances and with some good creative thinking, you could make it work for both parties. Then a lawyer would charge you around £2K for drafting the document.

The cash flow you receive from the property could be from zero if the owner is still living in the property and requires the transaction to move to a different property, but in this case, you wouldn't make any payments. Or it could be the cash flow expected for a buy to let as you would be covering the financial commitments for the property. It changes for each case.

CAPITAL GAINS

As you may be guessing, depending on the structure of the option, you would make good capital gains over certain a time (like the £20K above) or you could just charge a sourcing fee if you just decide to transfer the lease. It all depends on the difference in the price you negotiate and the perceived market value of the property.

And this is important here. The Perceived Market Value (PMV) of the property is not the same as the Open Market Value (OMV). This is the reason why some people will pay more in auctions for property (assuming they know what they are doing).

The PMV depends on the exit strategy which, in the eyes of the investor would increase the price that he or she would be willing to pay for the asset. For example, I am currently buying a spacious 2-bedroom 1 bathroom property which could have several exit strategies. One could be a single let to get £500 per month and another one could be converted to 4 bedrooms or even 6 bedrooms depending on how much I am willing to invest and use it for Service accommodation. For the 4-bedroom strategy, I calculate I could be getting £1200 per month and of the other one around £1500 with a 45% occupancy.

Even though in any case the valuation would be a brick and mortar one, the enhanced cash flow motivated me to £3K more when after the initial offer the vendor wanted a sealed bid from the four offers, she got.

That is what I mean by PMV, and if you want to transfer your Lease Option then you could package the deal for example as an HMO or conversion when the buyer can see the value. You could even go so far as to get planning permission for the modifications and then clearly have an edge on the sale you want to make.

COMPLEXITY

The complexity of this strategy comes I'd say, from being able to find people motivated enough to get into this type of agreement. You would require a good marketing system if you want to make this your main strategy or rely on your network or simply on chance.

Then you would need a lawyer, to ensure the deal makes financial sense and the use your Trusted Team to use for any of the strategies I've discussed in this book.

It depends on how complex you want to make it, you could just simply sell the option or packed it up so your gains can increase.

TIME

This strategy will mean you will need sellers and buyers if you want to use it for quick gains. That means a marketing system and that means a lot of time invested.

From then, as explained before, it will you more time depending on how much you are willing to squeeze the opportunity.

SALES AND MARKETING

This on its own would be an important chunk of time and effort from your side. You would need to be running two campaigns on two different fronts:

a. Your Sellers
b. Your Buyers

Then you would need to speak differently to each one as they are different profiles and target markets and do it consistently.

To create such a system, you would need to consider different advertisement channels such as social media, specialised publications, etc. and invest a good amount of money to create presence and built trust. Have you seen the advertisements for "We buy any house"? If so, that is exactly what I am talking about.

EXIT

The exit is to either keep the lease and exercise it or package it and sell it.

Either way requires looking into the best use of the asset so the transaction can create maximum profit. That is the reason why this tactic is not a bottom rung-type. It does require knowledge, a Trusted Team and financial skills to make it work.

KNOW-HOW

As an investor, I'd suggest you keep this tactic in your toolbox until you may need it, but focus mainly on others in this book unless you are willing to go all in.

This is especially true if you are in a market of sellers and not in one of the buyers as it is at the moment.

Always remember that in the property the Cash Cycle Speed is important and we should focus on those strategies that can help us speed up our portfolio growth and then use other tactics to support those fast-growth strategies.

Property investment in the UK, work and a pyramid where tactics, where you control properties of other investors, are located at the base and end up generating cash for the properties you own at the top. It truly is a very interesting process when you can see and enjoy the full picture in your portfolio.

FINAL WORDS

I've aimed to give you the bird's eye picture of property investment tactics. The different paths and tools you can take to have the financial muscle to be in a position of choice: To choose what to do with your time, to choose to create your own wealth and not others, to enjoy doing what you love even if that does make you any money because your property investments will make up for it.

The higher you go in the property ladder as I define it, the more personal growth you will require. Stretching yourself and working along with other investors and mentors is the faster way to get where you need. Once you know the rules of the game then it will truly turn into an exercise of how many assets you can own and control.

As I write these words, I've been just talking to German a close friend of mine who has gone on a 6-month holiday through Central America with no set-in-stone return date. He is not answering to anybody, he is not dependent on anybody. He has done his homework. He is free. Now he has to deal with a question few people in the world have to answer: What does he do with his time?

Average people are so busy trying to make ends that never have to face that question, which is a shame because at that location where you connect with your passion. The old question of 'What would you do if you had all the money you need?'

The funny thing is that many of us have worked hard in achieving such a state but don't prepare for success, in other words, we get unprepared to answer the "now what question". Anyway, it's a great question to have to answer.

As a final invitation, please come and join me at propertycashflow.co.uk. If there is any way I can help let me know, we can have a phone call or write to me at invest@propertycashflow.co.uk. It doesn't matter if you are just starting or are already working, I am always interested in connecting with you. With other investors.

On the pages that follow, I've given you four extra strategies that you may want to know about but they are what average investors would start with. Not a bad idea to know more about them but not essential. If you look at them from the investor's point of you in terms of creative schemes to configure your portfolio then you may detect some good models in the industry.

All the best in your financial journey.

Noel.

BONUS TACTICS

Some extra tactics, not so powerful but could be useful for beginners.

BONUS WAY NO. 1: RENT TO BUY

INITIAL CAPITAL	CASH FLOW	CAP. GAINS	C/XITY	TIME	SALES MARK.	EXIT	KNOW HOW

Type: Bottom Rung

The reason I write about this tactic is in case you want to start climbing the property ladder but are finding it very difficult to do so. There is always a way.

You Are Here

The Rent to Buy (R2B) is one of the UK's government's schemes to help first-time buyers into the property ladder. It works slightly different depending on whether you want to buy your property in London (there is known as Living Rent), other parts of England, Wales or Scotland.

In general, with R2B you would get a new property for 80% rent, of the market average and then you have up to five years to buy the property (time will vary per property), at the end of that time you either buy the property in full or part of it as in Shared Ownership, if neither of those options is taken, then you will have to move out.

INITIAL CAPITAL

R2B is designed in a way so you can save for the deposit for the property as you save in rent.

Let's say you save £200 rent per month by getting into R2B and you save that money for five years. That would be £12K you could have there for your property. Now, is not an obligation for you to save that money, but you are encouraged to do so, so you can get into the property ladder.

In London, the average rent you'd pay under this scheme is 33% below the market.

By the way, your household income will need to be less than £60K per year to be eligible for this scheme.

In terms of the price that you will pay for the property, it will be the market price, except for Wales where you would receive 50% of any increase in value of the property since you started your tenancy to use towards your deposit. If the property increased by £20K in 2 years then you'd get £10K towards your deposit. (By the way in Wales you pay the ongoing market rent, and if you want to buy you get 25% of the rent back towards your deposit.)

CASH FLOW

This is a tactic with no cash flow as you would be living in it and is not legal to sublet (unless you decide to go that route anyway).

This scheme is one designed to help those people who are struggling the most and therefore is expected that nobody would sublet.

CAPITAL GAINS

As an investor starting to climb the property ladder, your capital gains would come from what you save in rent (except for Wales) and the appreciation you get during the time you live in it after you've bought it.

You could try and do some refurbs to create more value but any changes would have to be agreed upon and approved by the housing association.

COMPLEXITY

The complexity of this tactic comes from actually finding a property because, as you may suspect, there is a lot of competition. In fact, R2B is not a scheme that is given a lot of publicity given the ratio offer/demand.

In general, you would need to have a good credit score, a household income of less than £60K per year and be able to provide proof of such income.

Thinking about it, I can see this is kind of a "lease option" but with the property price being the market average at the time of purchase.

TIME

Most time will be spent in finding a property that is suitably located for you, depending on where you work and where you want to live.

As you'd start living in the property through a Shorthold Assurance tenancy, as soon as you are approved then you could move in and start saving for it. If you live in London and looking for one of these, you could start your search here:

https://www.london.gov.uk/what-we-do/housing-and-land/homes-londoners/search

Once you get to the purchasing stage, you will need to engage your lawyers to ensure all searches are done, understand whether you are buying a freehold or a leasehold, flooding, etc.

There is no legal binding contract to buy the property, so if you don't like the conditions of sale then you just don't go for it.

SALES & MARKETING

As this is a social scheme, you only need to be able to "get lucky" and qualify so you can get it. As I said before these properties' availability are very limited.

EXIT

Once you own your property you can rent it out or sell it if you want. There is no legal requirement not to do so once it's yours.

The selling of the property would be done through the normal channels as the open market.

BONUS WAY NO. 2: SHARED OWNERSHIP

| INITIAL CAPITAL | CASH FLOW | CAP. GAINS | C/XITY | TIME | SALES MARK. | EXIT | KNOW HOW |

Type: Bottom Rung

Shared Ownership is another government scheme that has been implemented due to the increase in property value not being aligned with the increase in income. In simple terms, some areas in the UK have prices so ridiculously high that people can just afford to buy a fraction of the property only and share the ownership with a housing association, hence the name.

INITIAL CAPITAL

As I said, in this scheme, you can start by owning just a part of the property which normally is 25% and then you can scale up how much you own normally in chucks of 25% until you get to 100% ownership. So, if you have let's say £30K to put in property, you could be looking at buying a property of a maximum of £480K. This is how I arrived at this number:

£30K/0.25 = £120K (You have £30K and will own the 25% of the property so you share will be worth £120K).

£120K/0.25 = £480K (As £120K is 25% of the total value of the property you will be able to live in a £480K one).

This is to show that with this scheme, you are likely to have access to a bigger property thank if you buy through a normal process of a buy to let.

Just note I didn't include any fees that need to be paid in the process.

Bear in mind that you can get freehold or leasehold properties also on this scheme so ensure you are clear about what you are buying.

The whole point of Shared Ownership is to give access to people to at least own some property but as with all creative strategies, the result that the government wanted is probably not 100% what it was expected. More about that shortly.

CASH FLOW

This strategy won't give you any cash flow but will impact yours in two ways:

a. You will have to pay a mortgage in the, let's say, 25% you own and,

b. You will have to pay rent in the 75% the housing association owns.

So, for a property that costs about £650K at current rates you would be paying around £350 mortgage and £850 rent depending on the area and project. It depends on the area but I just wanted to give you an example so you have a feeling for how it works.

Effectively for the example above, you would be paying £1200 in total costs for a property that would be £2000 rental in market prices.

CAPITAL GAINS

I talked about the unexpected results of creative strategies. What I meant by that in relation to Shared Ownership is the fact that as you own a fraction of the property and prices continue to increase, you will like find yourself unable to buy the whole property and get stuck, depending on your income, at an ownership level of 50% or 75%.

Having said that, if you own let's say, 50% of the property and you want to sell it, you will get capital gains on your share.

The complication here is that to sell it you need to talk to the housing association and they have the first right to buy which could be a good or a bad thing depending on how long it takes them to find a buyer.

Remember I write about this strategy so you know what is available and in case you are trying to get into the property ladder at least to secure a place to live and then continue climbing.

COMPLEXITY

This tactic has a mid-level complexity if you take into account that only first-time buyers are allowed to get into this scheme, also, as of the time of writing, the combined income of the household should not be more than £90K. Also, the availability of properties under this scheme.

For a first-time buyer, the shared scheme could be daunting and the financial impact not be entirely understood if the investment is not clear, without taking into account any issues with the leasehold remaining in case the property being purchased is not brand new.

TIME

Time for this tactic is all about finding a property in a location that is useful for you and which you can afford. There are specialised websites that can be used to find or get into the waiting lists for housing associations. Then it would be the time so all the conveyancing is done correctly.

SALES AND MARKING

Pretty much none is required apart from your searching skills to find projects.

EXIT

As discussed before a property in this scheme can be sold getting your share of capital gains. By the same nature of the scheme and rules of the house associating these properties cannot be sublet or rented out.

KNOW-HOW

If this is the first rung of your property ladder climbing and you can't find another option, you could use it as a checkpoint as I call it so you can continue your advancement in your investment career.

As usual, you will be dealing with a conveyancing lawyer, a mortgage broker and the house association owning the project.

BONUS WAY NO. 3: BUYING OFF PLAN

INITIAL CASH CAP. C/XITY TIME SALES EXIT KNOW
CAPITAL FLOW GAINS MARK. HOW

Type: Middle Rung

This is one of the tactics used by people who want to invest in property without much risk and getting so additional appreciation without making too much of an effort.

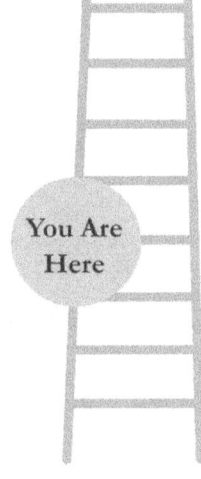

You Are Here

There are several different factors to consider when you're buying an off-plan property. So, if you are a professional property investor who is looking to get your returns as quickly as possible, this might not be the strategy for you to use. However, if you are a banker in the city, and you have some sort of like, bonus pay to you and you have some funds ready to invest, and but you don't have the time or skills to go and find properties to refurbish and can't bother using some of the high leverage tactics explained in this book, then obviously, this is probably the best option for you.

INITIAL CAPITAL

When buying an off-plan property, which has not been built yet you put in a 5% deposit and then eventually you pay the other 10 or 15% after a few months. It can take one or two years for the property to be ready at which point you can get a mortgage to secure the investment.

Selling off-plan and by stages is a good way builder of large projects have found to finance them. As one stage is finished, the properties in the one before will increase more in price benefitting those investors who got in first.

If you are unable to get a mortgage you may lose your deposit.

CASHFLOW

This investment tactic won't produce any cash flow until the property is ready for obvious reasons. But if you intend to rent it out, then your income will be whatever the market will pay for the type of asset you got.

CAPITAL GAINS

This strategy may be a good one for CGs if you choose a High Growth Area (HIGA) because is the market that will always dictate what you can sell for.

If you chose a HIGA where the average price from the time you pay your deposit to the time the property is completed, increases 20% that's what your CGs are going to be.

COMPLEXITY

The complexity of this tactic is relatively low. I'd say it comes from two places:

a. Ensuring the area, you are buying has an appreciation that meets your investment criteria.
b. Ensuring you are buying with a building company that has a good reputation for completing projects.

Understand that with this tactic you are kind of entering a joint venture where you lend money to the builder for one or two years with a promise of getting a property that can be mergeable so you can own your next asset.

Apart from that and the fact that you will only see drawings and a 3D rendering of what you are committing there is not much complexity here.

TIME

Depending on your exit strategy it will take more or less time. Let me explain.

If you are buying off-plan to live in it as I recently did with my flat near the Battersea area in London, then you probably know already where you want to buy but...

If you are buying to get some capital gains then your due diligence should be deeper to ensure you get the kind of returns you are looking for.

Also, the due diligence on the business you partner with to get the property built with low risk of the project running out of cash.

The process will involve visiting some model properties built to ensure buyers are more enticed to buy.

SALES AND MARKETING

If your exit strategy is to sell after buying take into account that your mortgage may stop you from doing so if it contains a no-sale clause for a certain amount of time (I've seen 6 months as a rule of thumb). So, if the flat took two years to build, 6 months no sale clause, plus another 4 to sell it, you'd be talking about an almost 3-year investment.

Personally, unless I am going to live in it, I wouldn't consider this tactic as part of my investment toolbox due to the long time it takes. It doesn't create **Money Speed.**

EXIT

So, you can sell it, rent it or live in it or all of it for several years.

The good thing is that you will have a brand-new building that won't require lots of maintenance and, if your due diligence was correct, will have a good demand and will go quickly.

It's important to be aware of the regulatory side of buildings and especially if buying flats which can affect your exit: One of the investors we work with, bought a property in Tottenham in London, rented it out and were in the process of selling but then the Grenfell Tower fire happened which rendered many flats unsellable (no lender would take the risk) until very expensive repairs are done.

As of the writing of this book, they are still waiting to know who will cover the costs.

KNOWHOW

This strategy is relatively easy to get into as long as you can put the financials together and understand the terms and conditions you are going into with the builder.

If you don't pay, you may face financial prosecution.

NOEL CARDONA –
WHO AM I ANYWAY?

www.propertycashflow.co.uk

'Property Investment Coach for the Elite'. Hi, I am Noel Cardona, when you work with me, I give you access to tested and proven strategies learned from my 10+ years as an entrepreneur, investor, author and speaker to accelerate your journey towards freedom, wealth and prosperity. I have been mentored by some of the best entrepreneurs in the world having access to cutting edge tools and lessons which the average failing entrepreneur will never get access to. People I don't normally work with are the negative thinkers, who are looking for approval and not advice, if you think that your business is different, then my advice won't work for you.

I am the most practical business mentor, coach, teacher you will ever meet. I am a plain-speaking, direct and upfront bloke who walks his talk and delivers on what he promises – EVERY time. If you are ready to take serious advice, contact me at info@propertycashflow.co.uk.

OTHER BOOKS BY NOEL

I have published seven books on entrepreneurship, personal growth and business excellence. If you want to see them all please go to *propertycashflow.co.uk.* While you are there join my list so we can start communicating continuously.

THE MENTAL BREAKFAST

The Mental Breakfast is a tremendous system for you to take charge of your own will and make your productivity go through the ceiling. There is so much more to increase your capacity to deliver than just playing the 'being busy' game. This book shows you the basics and also the method to be able to achieve two things. One, not to forget your dreams so you keep aligned and two, your alignment is maintained in the long term and not just for the first week of the year as happens to 99% of the population. This book talks about a breakthrough concept: Before you achieve Financial Freedom, you must achieve

Mental Freedom. I know for a fact that only a few people who read this book will have the courage to implement it! Will you be one of them?

INTENTIONAL WINNER

Intentional Winner shows you what the zero baseline for success is. It helps you understand how you need to think and act to start your journey to whatever you define as success. Also, it is a must-read for those who have been on this path for a while but don't seem to make any progress. Becoming an Intentional Winner requires knowledge of yourself and knowledge of a proven successful method that leads you faster towards your goals. Being successful is not necessarily becoming a millionaire; there are a lot more things to success than that. Intentional Winner talks about 5 drivers you need to learn and use to steer your life in the right direction.

www.ingramcontent.com/pod-product-compliance
Lightning Source LLC
Chambersburg PA
CBHW051529170526
45165CB00002B/664